Library of Congress Catalog Card Number: 62-13953
Printed in the United States of America

LET'S FIND OUT ABOUT
SUMMER

by

MARTHA and CHARLES SHAPP

Pictures by László Roth

FRANKLIN WATTS, INC.
575 Lexington Avenue, New York 22

There are four seasons in the year – fall, winter, spring, and summer.

There's the cool fall . . .

. . . and the cold winter.

There's the warm spring...

...and the hot summer.

When is summer?

Summer is when school is out.

Summer is vacation time.

Summer is when it's hot enough to go swimming.

Summer is the time for outdoor fun.

Summer days are very long.
Sometimes it's still light out when it's time for bed.

Summer days can be very, very hot.

On a very hot summer day, people like to be in the shade.

Sometimes in the summer, it's cooler indoors than it is outdoors.

You can cool the indoors.
You can't cool the outdoors.

Rain sometimes comes very suddenly in the summer.
Suddenly, dark clouds cover the sun.

Lightning flashes.
Thunder crashes.

The rain comes down.

Suddenly the rain stops.
The sun comes out.

Sometimes after a summer rain you can see a rainbow.

Summer is the time for growing.
The baby animals that were born in the spring...

. . . grow up in the summer.

The baby birds that were born in the spring...
...fly out of the nest in the summer.

The little tadpoles and fish that were born in the spring . . .

...grow big and strong in the summer.

Seeds that were planted in the spring...

...grow into fruits and vegetables.

Seeds that were planted in the spring . . .

...grow into summer flowers.

Insects seem to be everywhere in the summer.

On summer nights, you can see fireflies flashing in the dark.

Catch some fireflies in a jar.
Cover the jar.
Take the jar into a dark room and see the fireflies
light up.

There are four seasons in the year,
winter, spring, summer, fall.

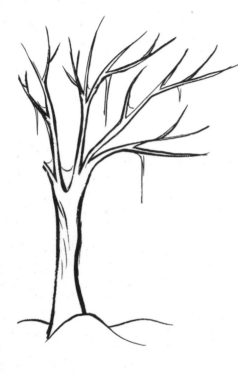

Don't you think that summer
is the best season of all?

VOCABULARY (99 words)

a
after
all
and
animals
are

baby
be
bed
best
big
birds
born

can('t)
catch
clouds
cold
comes
cool(er)
cover
crashes

dark
day(s)
don't
down

enough
everywhere

fall
fireflies
fish
flash(es)(ing)
flowers
fly
for

four
fruits
fun

go
grow(ing)

hot

in
indoors
insects
into
is
it('s)

jar

light
lightning
like
little
long

nest
nights

of
on
out
outdoor(s)

people
planted

rain
rainbow
room

school
season(s)

see
seeds
seem
shade
some
sometimes
spring
still
stops
strong
suddenly
summer
sun
swimming

tadpoles
take
than
that
the
there('s)
think
thunder
time
to

up

vacation
vegetables
very

warm
were
when
winter

year
you